Tales of the
SOUTHWOLD CANNONS

PETER KENT

"The Southwold Cannons are famous in our family. The children used to make a beeline for them as soon as they arrived in Southwold. They were better than any climbing frame. Later, I told them the history and they've been frightened of cannon balls ever since!"

MICHAEL PALIN

CUPOLA

On this map you can clearly see,
All of Southwold's artillery.
One to six are the biggest and best,
But you mustn't forget to sit on the rest.
Seven, eight and nine were the last to be fired,
Many years ago and now they're retired.
Ten is the one on which you cannot sit,
It's in the museum and there's only a bit.
Number eleven was once set in the quay,
It's scuffed, scarred and very rusty.

York Road
MUSEUM
Victoria Street
East Green
St James's Green
North Parade
HIGH STREET
Godyll Road
East Street
Queen Street
The Common
Gardner Road
Gun Hill
10
9
8
7
6
5
4
3
2
1

As part of his plan to protect England's coast,
King Henry sent cannons to places that needed them most.
Southwold got at least one, maybe more,
To defend the town in case of war.
For years this cannon stood guarding Sole Bay,
You can see a piece of it in the museum today.

For me, this firing is a first,
Please don't let the barrel burst.

Oh, my heart flutters! I'm full of fear.
I hope the bang won't hurt my ear.

King Henry's Cannon, 1545

Many years later Queen Elizabeth intended,
That Southwold should still be well defended.
She sent some guns, of iron and brass,
That fired at Spaniards sailing past.
The people were very glad to see,
Their shining, brand new artillery.

I hate guns. All noise and stinks.
I'd rather use my bow, methinks.

God bless her gracious majesty,
For saving us from the enemy.

Armada Artillery, 1588

Forty years on the cannons were neglected,
As no attack from the sea was expected.
Then a pirate ship came and bombarded the town,
The gunners fired one shot and then lay down.
As cannon balls whistled in from the bay,
The gunners gave up and all ran away.

I must be brave and face the foe,
But I'm trembling from hat to toe.

It's too late now to dig a hole,
Oh, how I wish I was a mole.

Pirate Attack! 1626

Dutch and English fleets had a fight in the bay,
Hundreds of ships fired at each other all day.
The blast of the cannons was thunderously loud,
Gunpowder smoke made enormous clouds.
The battle ended with the setting sun,
But nobody knew which fleet had won.

There's not much point in firing a shot.
No one will notice amongst all this lot.

Down with the English! I hate them so much,
But we shall beat them because we're Dutch.

The Battle of Sole Bay, 1672

When England was again at war,
French ships sailed close to the shore,
Sinking English ships, just as they pleased.
The townsfolk were helpless and very aggrieved.
Their ancient old cannons were eaten by rust,
The carriages all rotten and crumbling to dust.

O what a disaster! It makes me sick,
When all I can do is shake my stick.

We need new guns, our town to defend,
Otherwise these attacks will never end.

Pirates Again! 1745

We need new cannons the townsfolk agreed,
Let's write to the king and hope we succeed.
King George looked at his cannons in store,
And decided that Southwold deserved some more.
He sent six new cannons to stand on Gun Hill,
All were delighted 'til they got the bill.

With these new guns we have nothing to fear.
No enemy now will dare to come near.

I hope we don't have to fire them a lot.
I've had to pay for the powder and shot.

New Cannons, 1746

In 1822 King George the Fourth,
Sailed past Southwold on his way up north.
The townsfolk waved flags and began to sing,
Then decided to fire a salute for the king.
But this loyal celebration was all a great flop,
For the king was annoyed and told them to stop.

What's that dreadful din? It doesn't please me.
I want to be calm and quiet at sea.

Don't worry, sire, we shall soon have sailed past.
But if you so wish, I will give them a blast.

The Grumpy King, 1822

Queen Victoria's baby gave joy to the nation,
Southwold fired its old cannons in celebration.
A happy crowd came to cheer and see,
The salute which, alas, was a tragedy.
An untrained gunner loaded powder too fast,
And perished in a sudden, fiery blast.

Well, well! That is indeed a puzzle,
That he should stand so near the muzzle.

Now the cannons must be retired.
It's the last time they can be fired.

Tragedy, 1842

In Victorian times the cannons were a fixture,
In every family's summer holiday picture.
The cameras were heavy and made out of wood,
The photographer looked at the scene 'neath a hood.
You had to sit still. You could not stir.
If you moved just a little your face was a blur.

It's very hard sitting still to pose,
When I've an itching, twitching nose.

I can hear a wasp, or is it a bee?
Whatever it is, it mustn't sting me.

Holiday Photos, 1880

In 1917 the Germans thought,
The six old cannons made Southwold a fort.
They sent two ships to bombard the town,
Smashing windows and tumbling chimneys down.
The townsfolk, frightened of another attack,
Buried the cannons in case the Germans came back.

Why can't we just hide them in a shed?
It looks like we're burying something dead.

We'll dig them up at the end of the war,
Southwold will have its cannons once more.

Cannons Buried, 1917

George Orwell's real name was Eric Blair.
He had a weird moustache and very thick hair.
He came to Southwold after writing a book,
About being a tramp and a French cook.
Eric claimed he was tall as a cannon was long,
But this photograph proves that he was wrong.

I say, mummy, is that man a tramp,
Sleeping on a cannon 'cos the grass is damp?

No, no darling. That's the Blair's only son.
I think it's his idea of having fun.

George Orwell, 1934

At the beginning of the Second World War,
The six old cannons were put in store.
In their place were two big guns,
Camouflaged and weighing tons.
They weren't fired often, they made such a bang.
All windows cracked and every ear rang.

I say, girls and boys, now stop your game!
That's coastal artillery not a climbing frame.

Oi! You kids! Get off my gun.
It's not a toy. It's not for fun.

The Second World War, 1943

Three hundred years after the Battle of Sole Bay,
Southwold decided to celebrate the day.
Three rusty old cannons were found in a yard,
Volunteers cleaned them and worked very hard.
They learnt to fire them with correct army drill,
And gave the crowds watching a very loud thrill.

I've been trained and know what do.
Not like the poor chap in 1842.

I've forgotten to put my earplugs in,
But I must be brave and try to grin.

Battle Celebrations, 1972

To wash out the barrel you must remember,
There might still be a smouldering ember.

The bag of black gunpowder goes in first,
Not too much in case the barrel bursts.

Ram the powder down as hard as you can,
The tighter it's packed, the louder the bang.

In goes the cannon ball, also called a round,
It's made of iron and weighs nine pounds.

Ram it down firmly and then a rope clout,
To stop the cannon ball rolling out.

Fill the vent with gunpowder fine,
Take aim so your target is in line.

With your match burning bright but slow,
Touch the powder and the cannon will BLOW!

Parts of a Cannon

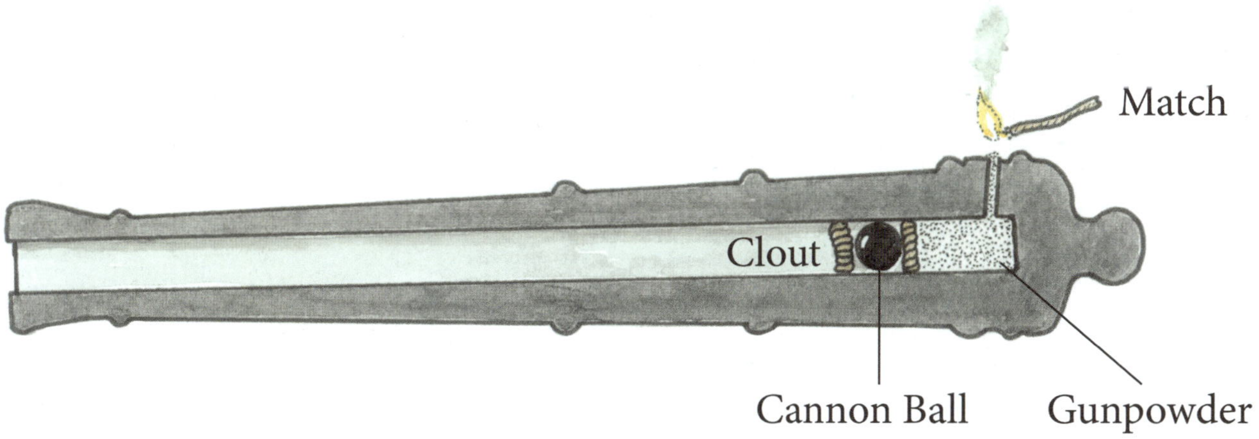

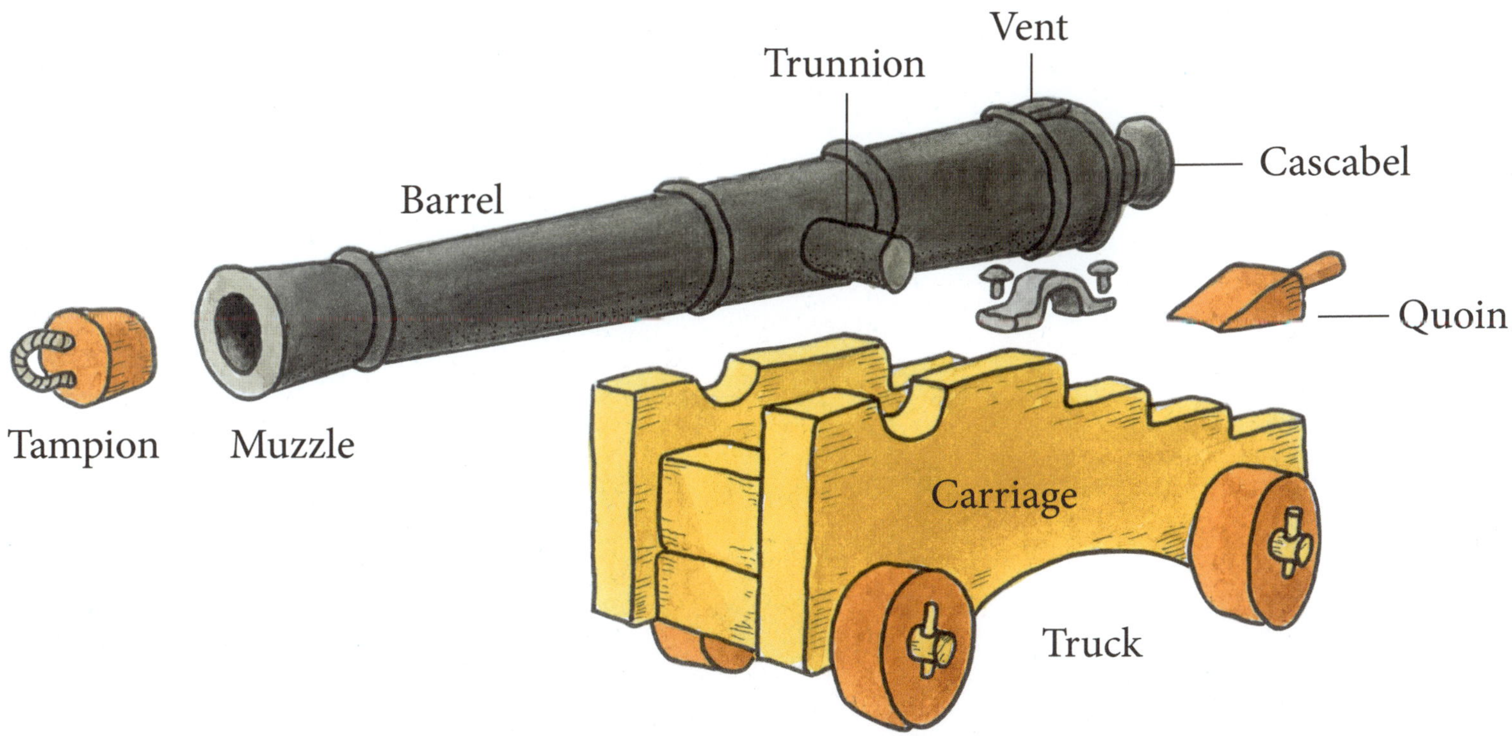

For centuries the cannons have stood on Gun Hill,
As long as there's Southwold, they'll be there still.
Their only job now is to provide a prop,
For family photos with the children on top.

Children who complain that it's all a bore,
Are told that it's the local cannon law.
Those who were pictured in monotone,
Snap their grandchildren on a smart phone.

Stick your
photo here